Trail to

Leadership

A Leadership Fable for New and Rising

Leaders

Luke Crane

DEDICATION

To my wife, Renée, and my loving family.

CONTENTS

CHAPTER 1

THE PERFECT COMPANY

I didn't ask for this. I simply did what my dad taught me as a kid. I can still hear his voice in my head to this day. "Always work hard Paul, always do right by people, good things will come." I hated it when I was a kid, but now I know he was giving me a gift.

I went to a smaller state college. It was not my first pick, but I didn't exactly have the GPA for Yale. I worked to make good grades in my classes. I kept to myself. It isn't that I was bad with people, it is just that big crowds drain me. I did reasonably well in my studies, but I also didn't graduate top of my class. Some might call me a 'middle of the crowd' kind of guy.

Some of my earliest memories were building things with Legos. My parents would call my room the minefield due to the large amount the small pieces on the floor. As I grew older, I challenged myself to build more elaborate projects. Eventually, I was doing them without the instructions. I studied mechanical engineering. It was kind of a no brainer.

I graduated and joined the working class right out of college. Back then I was eager to make money. I washed dishes and built websites for side money. After a couple of entry level positions that actually used the degree that I paid money for, I learned what I liked and did not like in a company's mission and culture. Eventually, I found the golden goose of employers. I mean this company was fantastic in every way. I knew that this was where I wanted to build my career. After six interviews, even one with the president of the company, I finally landed a position. So I took my dad's advice. I hunkered in, worked hard, and did right by people.

That outstanding company is Aeromic Aviation Inc. Sounds like a candle company doesn't it? I thought so too when I saw their name for the first time. In reality, it is a mid-sized company based out of Pittsburg with around 150 employees. We specialized in the materials and formation of aircraft wings and parts. With some big contracts and a flair for innovation, Aeromic is doing well culturally and financially.

I know engineering wings doesn't sound glamorous, but for someone like me, I am a kid in a candy shop. Or a video game fanatic with unlimited quarters in the world's biggest arcade. Or a . . . well you get the idea. I get to work on things as little as fittings and as big as new, groundbreaking, aerodynamic 3D models.

I'll never forget my first day. I could not stop smiling to save my life. I didn't care if my title had the word "analyst" in it. I was living the dream. If that wasn't a big indicator of my enthusiasm, then my interaction with the president of the company sure was. I talked so much he must have thought I was the worst hire on earth. I was so amazed that the president of the company would take the time to welcome me and have a conversation on my first day. It was unforgettable.

My dad's words were right. I was at A.I. for 13 months before my first promotion. You should have seen my parents smile when I told them over dinner about my promotion. A new set of business cards later, and I was a full-fledged engineer. Then just short of my 3-year anniversary, I was promoted to Sr. Engineer. I even got an office!

That feels like such a long time ago, but for now . . . . . . I AM IN WAY OVER MY HEAD.

CHAPTER 2

THE ANNOUNCEMENT

It was 2PM on Friday when Dave came into my office. Dave was a bigger guy. He had one of those body shapes that you know he is fit, but probably still downs an order of fries and a chocolate milkshake every once in a while. Dave is my manager. He is actually the best one I have ever seen. Everyone loves Dave. One time he flippantly joked that he was leaving in a meeting, and three people later told me they got their resumes ready to apply wherever he was going. He is that good. One of the things I love about Dave is you can always tell his mood. If he is smiling, things are good because he is almost always smiling. If he is not smiling, then something is seriously wrong.

Dave sat down in my only visitor chair that my mom and dad gave me as a new office gift. My mom believed comfy chairs made happy conversation. Dave had a huge grin on his face. That wasn't unusual. As I said, Dave was always smiling. But there was something different about this smile. I couldn't put my finger on it. Maybe it was something in his eyes. There was a hint of excitement and at the same time mischief.

He started talking almost as soon as he sat down. He always got to the point with things and didn't like wasting time. That took some getting used to at first. Most people like to chat about the weather or their golf game before getting to the real stuff. Dave preferred to skip the pleasantries. He didn't have a booming voice, but he wasn't soft spoken either. It was a confident calmness. He rarely raised his voice except in excitement ---- never in anger.

In his excited voice he said, "Paul… I'm about to share some exciting news."

I thought "This should be interesting."

I started to roll around the numerous theories in my head of what would come next. Were we going to get that big contract overseas? Would that mean travel? I have always wanted to visit China! The culture fascinated me, and they produce some of the top engineering minds in the world. I wonder how long we will be there? I will need to find a home for my Betta fish, but that shouldn't be hard. Will he be coming too? I don't know if I want to go without him. I love Chinese food, but I have read that it is different when you are actually there?

I was so lost in my own thoughts about foreign adventures that I almost missed Dave's words completely.

"I'm announcing my retirement."

I was just thinking, "I wonder if I still know how to use chopsticks" when the words hit me.

There was a considerable pause… Did I really just hear what I think I heard?

"Well. . . that's great Dave," I managed to squeeze out. "Congratulations… really."

It was lackluster at best, and we both knew it. Why would he tell me this was exciting news? This is anything but exciting!

He went on. "We have done some great work together and I have poured my heart and soul into this company. Over the last couple of years, I have poured my heart and soul into you, Paul."

I can't believe Dave is leaving me. Mentally, I chastised myself. "Dave isn't leaving *you* stupid, he is leaving the company… It is not all about you." I just couldn't wrap my head around it.

A thousand questions rushed through my mind. "Why? When? How long do you have? Wait, that makes it sound like he is dying!" Would he be sitting on a beach in Maui sipping a Mai Tai and snorkeling on the coral reefs in 3 months… 2 months… next week? I needed answers.

Obviously, I am devastated by this news. Dave is one of the reasons I love this company so much. He is vibrant, encouraging, tough at times, but he always knows how to inspire me and move me to do my best work. I remember how he welcomed me to the team on my first day with his big grin and a very firm handshake. He taught me everything I know. . . and now he is leaving.

I was just about to say "thank you" to his attempt at encouraging me when he continued. "I have already talked to the guys upstairs and we are all in agreement . . . you are the perfect fit for my replacement."

I was staring at my desk. You know that feeling when you are happy and sad at the same time. When I thought about the opportunity to move up in the company, I felt like I was on top of the world. Then, in almost the same thought, Dave was not going to be there, and a deep pit appeared in my stomach. For the next few moments I went back and forth between emotions. After snapping out of my mixed emotional state, I realized that Dave was staring at me.

"I'm sorry," I said shaking my head, "I guess it is just a lot to take in. I have so many questions."

Dave broke the ice. It was like he was reading my mind. He was good at that. He could always size up a situation in an instant and know what others were feeling.

"You are probably wondering how long I have left."

"Yes."

"And you are probably wondering if you can actually do this job."

"Yes."

He laughed and raised an eyebrow, "And you are probably wondering if you will get my office and a pay raise."

"NO!" Dave looked at me with a smile that said he knew better, "I mean yeah... but no!" I said nervously.

"I'm just giving you a hard time Paul" he said without skipping a beat. "There will be a lot more questions I'm sure but let me get ahead of those." He paused as I leaned in.

"I have 3 months left. The announcement is going out tomorrow for my retirement and, *if you say yes*", he emphasized the words and smirked, "then your announcement will go out with it."

I just realized that I had not given him an answer. Had he really asked a question?

"Are you sure?" I asked. "I mean I'm pretty young and there are people who have been here much longer than me."

He grinned, "So you are saying no?"

"No" I said back quickly.

"Okay, so no it is." He started to get up and turn for the door.

"Wait . . . that's not what I meant. Yes. Yes I will replace you . . ." Really. Did I just say that? "I mean." I composed myself, "I will take the opportunity. Thank you." At least that one sounded somewhat professional.

As he turned, I could see his smile had widened even further, and I knew he was having fun with this whole thing.

"Well alright! As for the other questions, yes you can do this job and I'm going to help. Yes, you get my office but I'm taking my chair. I love that chair! And yes . . . it comes with a pay raise."

"Wow" was all I could say.

"Yes wow!" He replied. "Now there is a lot still to learn and only a few short months to learn it."

"Your right. Maybe we could schedule some time . . ." Dave interrupted me with a wave of his hand as he walked toward the door.

"We are going to do things a little differently." He squinted his eyes in thought. "Have you ever been backpacking?" I got ready to respond with a resounding

NO when he interrupted. "Never mind, don't answer that. We start tomorrow morning at 8AM. . . my house." And then he was gone.

I sat there for a full five minutes. I got excited. Then I got scared. "How was I going to replace someone like Dave?" This cycle happened over and over for the next few hours as the day wound to a close.

As I packed up my stuff, something was nagging me about how the conversation ended with Dave, "What does backpacking have to do with Dave leaving?"

CHAPTER 3

THE CHOICE

I had absolutely no idea what to expect. Why were we meeting at his house? I had never seen Dave's house. Is it big? As my mind began to wander, I was struck with a thought. "Where in the world am I?" The road was a pothole nightmare and getting narrower. I would catch a break and speed up, only to slow down again at the next gaping crater in the road. Now I knew what the tortoise felt like in the race against the hare. I checked the address that Dave texted me twice before I left so I knew I was going in the right direction at least. The kind, and slightly judgmental, British voice of my GPS told me to take a left. What left? All that I see are trees and what looks like a dirt trail leading into the woods. My only saving grace indicating that there was a home at the other end of the "trail" was a lone wooden mailbox with the address on the side. I slowly pulled in and mentally prepared myself.

After 100 feet of feeling like Goldilocks on the way to grandma's house, the trees opened to a large, sloping green field. Perched at the top was the house. Anticipating a larger traditional home, I was surprised and a little confused to find a modest A-frame log cabin. It had a green roof and full wrap around porch, I could only think, "this would be an amazing Airbnb."

I pulled into the driveway in between Dave's gold Toyota Camry and the dirtiest Jeep Wrangler I think I have ever seen. "Had Dave invited someone else?" I spotted Dave in the garage digging through three large boxes. He looked up from one of them and waved me into the garage with what looked like a pair of short javelins in his hand. He had on blue jeans and a faded James Taylor T-Shirt. I suddenly felt way overdressed in my slacks and a buttoned-down dress shirt. I knew Dave could not resist a little ribbing, so I mentally braced for the comments that were to come.

"Welcome to Casa De Viajes," Dave said with a slight Spanish accent. Then he pointed to the far wall with the javelin. A faded cut slat of cedar with chipped white paint confirmed the name: House of Journeys.

"Thanks!" I said enthusiastically. "I really like your cabin. Is it technically a cabin or a house?"

Before he had a chance to answer his eyes locked onto my outfit. "Thank you Paul . . . I really like your… socks." A sly grin revealed itself in slow motion. I realized I was wearing my favorite pair of "unique" socks. My fashionable friend Zach told me loud socks were in for a person of my age, so I bought a couple of pairs. This particular pair had a light blue background with monkeys dressed up in suits. Get it . . . monkey suit?

It was my turn to give a little jab. "I know what you're thinking, but if I had known, I would have dressed more like a band groupie too."

Dave responded by an over exaggerated clutch to his chest like he had been hit by an arrow, and we both laughed. Ice broken.

Dave stopped rummaging and motioned me to sit at a white fold out table with two matching chairs. As usual, he got straight to the point. "So, tell me, why are you here Paul?" The question seemed vague, but with the long car ride, my mind had time to prepare.

"I'm here to learn" was my predetermined answer. I smiled and mentally patted my back for my preparedness.

Dave responded, "Good answer." Then he paused like he was looking for more.

"Crap!" I said to myself.

The silence became crushing before I responded again.

Dave didn't seem bothered. He was always good at silence in a conversation. "I'm here because . . . I want to be a leader like you." It was true. A little brown nosing, but true.

"Ah, a leader." Dave nodded. "So, you have made the choice."

"Yes" I said, with mild confusion about the word choice.

Dave went on because he knew what I needed. "Paul, all great journeys start with a choice. Consider some of the greatest journeys of the past. Columbus made the choice to explore new lands, *then* rallied the support and funding to make it happen. Lewis and Clark made the choice to trail west across unknown terrain and *then* they inspired 45 people to join them on the journey. It sounds like you, Paul, have made the choice to start your leadership journey. It is the first step, and the most important step, in every leader's life."

I thought for a moment. "Yea. I have made the choice."

"And now that you have made the choice," Dave got up and pulled two aluminum framed backpacks from behind a box, "it is time to prepare for the journey."

Paul smiled, "have you ever been backpacking Paul?"

"Are you serious?" I asked. I was hoping this was another analogy.

"Yes . . .you know, taking a backpack and hiking into

the woods with just your supplies and yourself for a couple of days." Dave explained it as if I had never heard of the term.

"I know what it is, and no. I have never been much of an outdoors guy."

"Well that is going to change in 4 short weeks. You and I are headed to a beautiful section of the Appalachian Trail called Blue Mountain right here in Pennsylvania. A beautiful journey to teach you more about your leadership journey."

I quickly understood that this was not an analogy. I didn't know how I felt. My idea of the outdoors was smores in the oven, not a full-blown Survivor Man scenario. "Okay…." I said worriedly.

"Now we have some work to do and it starts now. Don't worry, your slacks won't get dirty, and I have all the gear taken care of." Dave grinned, "We are going to start prepping for the journey."

"Now?"

"Now."

In true Dave fashion, we dove right into it. First, he had me pull out and organize two of everything: headlamps, hiking poles (remember the small javelins), sleeping bags, water bottles. The list went on and on. It's like Dave was a walking REI store. While I was organizing in two's, Dave was grabbing one thing after another ---- Some kind of pump thing, a bag of wood shavings, a tent and a small bag with a red tank of some sort, a map and a compass. The compass definitely caught my eye. It was solid metal with a gold finish. The edges were scratched, and the gold was worn off where you grip it in your hand. You could tell it definitely had many years of use. He held it in his hand for a moment, opening and closing the top, before placing it on the table. You could tell it held great value to Dave.

After packing was all over, I was beginning to wonder if this was one of Dave's jokes to get me to organize his garage. Like some kind of twisted leadership lesson for not blindly following instructions, but I soon found out ----it wasn't.

I then started the process of negotiations. I negotiated a great deal on a car last month, so I was hopeful this would work. "Dave, I don't know if I can do the whole thing." It was not a strong start, but I needed him to know that I was not ready.

"You probably don't think you are ready," said Dave.

How does he do that? A brief moment I thought he was a real-life Jedi. Next, he was going to wave his hands and say, "You will do this," and I would be powerless to resist.

"I don't just *think* Dave, I *know* I'm not ready."

"Just to be clear, which 'thing'," he air quoted, "aren't you ready for?" He looked at me for a moment. It was one of those uncomfortable stares. It is fine at first, and then when the eye contact isn't broken, you feel like they are seeing much more of you than you would like. He smiled knowingly and said, "I wasn't ready either, but I made the choice, and it wasn't an option any more for me."

My negotiation wasn't working. I needed a new angle. "Dave, I don't have enough vacation to spend on however many days we are going."

"That has already been taken care of."

"Of course it has" I thought. That was my last effort at negotiations. I could feel something in my mind change. My mental barrier had given way to the idea that I was going. I guess Dave would call it making a choice. It must have been obvious on my face because Dave got up and unfolded a worn map on the table and motioned me to sit down again. The journey had begun. "All of this is for a purpose Paul. I want you to keep this in mind as we move forward. You said you aren't ready, right? I think you meant you aren't ready to lead more than you aren't ready to go backpacking."

He had me there.

"We are going to use this outdoor journey to teach you about the leadership journey. The more you can connect the dots there . . . the more ready you will be."

"So you are a Jedi!" I wanted to yell, but felt that would

have been a bit inappropriate.

Dave said, "The first thing you need to know about the journey is that it starts with preparation. Have you ever met someone who went headlong into something difficult without preparing?"

"Yes." I said.

"How did it turn out for them?"

"Let's just say they learned a valuable lesson." I was thinking of me as a Senior in High School. I tried out for the wrestling team to impress a girl --- Renee. No training. No preparations. Just blind love. I realized the hard way, and very quickly, that wrestling takes much more than I was ready to give.

"So, let's not make the same mistake."

We spent the next hour looking over the map. Dave explained to me the importance of preparing the path ahead. We looked at the trail and plotted our distances between potential campsites. Dave made sure to explain to me that the lines on the topographical map were changes in elevation and how it might look like a short distance on a piece of paper, but in reality, we would be climbing 800 feet in elevation. We also looked for water sources along the way to refill water bottles and our point of entry and exit.

Next, I found out that Dave was not getting me to clean his garage but had a detailed list of supplies that we would need. Some things we needed two of, like water bottles and flashlights, but some things we would share, like a stove and tent. We put together a packing list and distributed things evenly. Well, actually Dave probably took on more than me in reality, but I wasn't about to point that out. Knowing Dave, I'm sure he did it on purpose.

After the preparations were set, Dave said, "There are two more things we need to talk about."

By now I was starting to embrace the process and said, "Okay."

"The first is that despite all this planning and preparing, we will never be able to account for everything."

"Uhhhh . . . what do you mean?" What I wanted to say was, "Why are we doing all this then?"

"We can put things down on paper all day. We can plan routes and hypothesize about every detail, but until we get out there . . . we just don't know."

"Comforting." I said sarcastically.

"I know," Dave said with his own sarcastic flair. "Leadership is like that too. Do you think I know exactly what is going to happen before it does? Far from it. I can be as prepared as I can and after that . . . ." He stopped and shrugged his shoulders.

"You roll with the punches," I finished.

"Exactly. Once you accept that you won't be prepared

for everything, you are prepared. . . to not be prepared."

I got it. Be mentally prepared that you can't account for everything. "And the second thing?" I asked.

Laughing as he said it, "You need to start walking everywhere. Ideally with a backpack that has weights in it. If you don't, this particular journey is going to kick your butt!"

On the drive home I had more time to think. Dave said that I needed to connect the dots. What parts of this could be connected to leading people? Once I hit civilized roads, I pulled over to get gas and jotted down some notes.

Preparing for the Journey

1. The journey begins with a choice - The choice to start the leadership journey is the first step. I am the only one who can make that choice.

2. Preparing for the leadership journey - before you take the action, you need to prepare. Prepare as much as you can. Plot, plan, list and account for as much as possible.

3. You cannot account for everything in leadership, so do not expect you will be totally prepared. expect to. Be ready to not be ready.

CHAPTER 4

BEGINNINGS

I felt like I had time. Lots of time actually. I know Dave said "four short weeks" when we were at his house, but what I didn't realize was that he put the word *short* in there for a reason. IT COMPLETELY FLEW BY.

At Dave's instruction, I started walking more. I even dusted off my old college backpack and filled it with some engineering text books that I had lying around collecting dust. At least those got one more use after college.

Two things were constantly on my mind. First, do people die on the Appalachian Trail? Second, are there bears? So, I did what I thought was best… I did an online search. That was a very bad idea. Of course, the only thing that showed up in the search were all the people who had died on the trail and how many bear attacks were reported with gruesome detail. I won't even start on the image search.

I immediately sent the results to Dave in hopes he would call the whole thing off. Not surprisingly, he simply said he had it covered. I wanted to respond, "Tell me how you have wild bears and death covered Dave!" But I didn't. I reminded myself of something Dave said in his garage, "All great journeys start with a choice."

Four weeks passed like four hours and before I knew it, Dave and I were in his mud coated Jeep headed for the trailhead. Dave truly had taken care of the time off dilemma. It turns out he convinced them that this was the same as an offsite conference, and I would be getting paid while backpacking. They would even reimburse me for the costs of food and any supplies. With that knowledge I purchased the one thing Dave told me I needed to get, a good pair of hiking boots.

We pulled up to the trailhead, and I was already feeling out of my element. I guess a life spent in the concrete jungle doesn't quite prepare you for the great outdoors. We got out of the Jeep, and I unboxed my brand-new purchase. Dave looked at me with a frown. Dave never frowns so I knew I was in trouble.

"Paul, I told you to get hiking boots 3 weeks ago."

I replied, "I did."

"I also told you to make sure you wear them before we started."

"I wore them at the store, and they fit well. Why . . . what did I do wrong?" I had a feeling this wasn't good.

Dave said, "I meant wear them to break them in."

"Awesome," I thought. "Starting off with a win. How bad could it be?"

We spent the next half hour going through our list one last time. After it all checked out, we re-packed our backpacks and put them on. "Holy crap this is heavy" I thought to myself. Instead of showing weakness I said, "What a beautiful day." Dave looked at me and smiled. "Yes it is." He closed his eyes and took a deep breath in through his nose. "Yes it is." Then we took our first steps on to the trail.

1. Clarifying directions

    a. Make sure you ask.

    b. Make sure you understand.

    c. Always seek full understanding.

2. Time

    a. Do not assume you have all the time you need.

    b. Time is the one thing you can fully control.

CHAPTER 5

THE TRAIL

The hike started out well. My pack took some adjusting for the first mile. Dave said it was important to put the weight of the pack on my hips and use the shoulder straps to keep it close to my back. I didn't understand at first, but then I started to feel the strain in my shoulders. I asked for a quick break, tightened my waist straps, and felt immediate relief. I thought, "Maybe this won't be so bad."

The landscape was absolutely breathtaking. We almost immediately entered what I would consider a canopy of rhododendron. No, I didn't know what they were called, but Dave pointed them out with a small warning not to burn them for firewood because they were poisonous, and the smoke would not be pleasant. How did he know all this stuff? It fascinated me that he was a very talented engineer in his own right yet had vast knowledge of the outdoors.

We were about a mile in when I decided to strike up conversation. "How long have you been backpacking for Dave?"

He quickly replied, "Since I was a boy."

His voice was quick and to the point. Did he not want to talk? I decided to try again with a different angle. "What is the furthest you have gone?" I was genuinely interested.

Another quick reply, "After college I did the entire Appalachian Trail."

"Oh!" I was impressed. "So you really like this stuff?"

He simply nodded in reply. I felt like I was in high school again, and the cool crowd was putting up with me out of necessity. I decided to keep quiet, but deep down it really bothered me that Dave didn't want to talk. What kind of teacher doesn't talk! After all, I agreed to this thing because he said he was going to teach me about being a leader. I remember an Abe Lincoln quote, "Better to be silent and thought a fool than to speak out and remove all doubt." So, I let my anger brew in silence.

I was lost in my frustration of the silent treatment when my brand-new boots caught the first rock. Normally I am quite good on my feet, but with the 38 pounds of gear and food on my back, let's just say my center of gravity was less centered and more gravity. I fell . . . hard. Dave stopped and asked if I was okay. He offered his hand to help. Thankfully it was just a case of wounded pride rather than wounded body part. Out of frustration I refused the hand and was back on my feet in less than three minutes. I wanted him to feel my frustration a bit. After a mental body assessment, I was putting one foot in front of the other once again, albeit much more cautiously.

It took another near fall to adjust my focus. I no longer allowed my mind to wander to my frustration and comfort. I had made an important observation. Dave wasn't falling. So logically If I do what he does, I won't fall. I focused my full attention on Dave. Slowly, I started to see that he was making it obvious where I should step. I started to pay more attention to how Dave was moving and what he was doing. It took me another mile to realize that when there was a rock or root protruding from the ground, Dave would tap it twice with his hiking pole before stepping over it. Why didn't he just tell me that to begin with! My frustration grew hot. Was this his idea of leadership? I was only relieved by one thing ---- I was starting to get the hang of it.

It was like a dance. Constantly reading what Dave was doing and adjusting accordingly. He would slow down, and I would slow down. He upped the pace and I would . . . well . . . try to keep up. I started to notice when he would look left and right. He wasn't merely enjoying the scenery. it almost felt as if he was telling me to enjoy the bird in the tree to the right or the view over the ledge to the left. After a while, it became second nature . . . in nature. I just wish he would say something!

Everything hurt. I mean everything. Muscles I didn't know existed hurt. The air hurt. Okay, maybe not the air, but that is what it felt like. I was more relieved when Dave said, "This looks like a good spot for camp" than I had ever been in my entire life. Dave turned around to see how I was doing, and I did the only thing I could think of, I acted like I was not even winded. Outward I was a picture of strength and poise. Inward I was a picture of a hospital emergency room. Pain upon pain layered with pain. To top it all off, my aggravation at Dave's lack of communication was at an all-time high.

"Let's put our packs down here and start to set up camp." Dave said.

"Sounds good!" I replied, with more relief in my voice than I wanted. Dave just smiled and got to work.

After a quick walk around, we found a good spot for the tent, and I learned something valuable. You don't want to put your tent under, or in the path of, a dead tree. Dave called them "widow-makers." I am not married, but I got the point.

Dave got the fire going, and I was tasked with setting up the tent. "This should be easy," I thought. "After all, I am an engineer." Reality check ---- it was not! I have put together Ikea furniture that made more sense than that tent. After assembling the entire tent, I realized I had forgotten the rain fly and basically had an existential crisis. All I wanted to do was throw the poles in the woods and burn the rest. A brief disassembly and reassembly and the it was finally finished. I stood back to admire my accomplishment. Dave still hadn't said a word.

The time must have gotten away from me. As I was putting the sleeping bags in the tent, my stomach angrily growled. It had obviously smelled dinner before my mind could process the information. I was somewhat grateful that Dave had gone ahead and made dinner, but that didn't make up for the silent treatment he was clearly giving me.

Dehydrated food in a bag never tasted so good. I think I had spaghetti with meatballs. Or was it lasagna? I was perplexed at how you can add boiling water to a bag and come out with such an amazing meal. It made no difference to me, because it was down the hatch before I read the label. I looked up from my empty bag to see Dave smiling. "Hungry?" he chuckled.

"Yes." It was my turn to give some short replies.

His next question was more pointed, "How are you

feeling after today?"

I had a feeling he knew the answer to that question, but I wasn't going to let my facade die so quickly. "Great!" I said with faked enthusiasm. "I guess this backpacking thing isn't that hard." What I really wanted to say was, "You're going to have to stuff me in that pack for the rest of the trip because I can't walk another step." But I didn't.

After dinner we washed our spork/knife combo tools and put the empty bags in a large Ziplock. I wanted to ask Dave why we don't just burn them in the fire, but I decided to apply Abe's quote again and remain silent. Plus, I didn't know if I could keep my composure in conversation right now.

Dave walked to his pack and returned to the fire with 2 small notebooks. He handed one to me. It was actually pretty cool. In the spine of the notebook, it had a small square pen that fit perfectly inside. I opened it up and found my name on the first page next to the word "Owner."

"Don't write in it yet. I find it nice to write down my thoughts right before I go to bed."

I held up the notebook. "Thanks."

Dave went right into it. "What did you experience today?"

"Oh, now you want to talk" I thought. What kind of a broad question was that? I tersely replied, "There is a lot.

Where should I start?"

"Wherever you want."

"I . . . well . . . I don't know." I could feel my face getting hot in frustration. First, you don't talk to me for almost 6 miles of hiking and now you expect me to be chatty Cathy?

"Something on your mind?" Dave sat smiling as if he didn't see it.

"Fine! You really want to know? I tried to start a conversation with you while we were hiking, and you acted like I was your little brother that you put up with taking to school. I thought I came out here to learn and all I did was follow you around for 6 miles of silence. Is that what you wanted to hear?" It came out a lot rawer than I intended, but what did he expect?

"Wow. So you think we didn't communicate?"

"No! Communication involves talking. You know, that thing you do with your mouth?" I was fully aware how disrespectful it sounded.

Curiously calm, Dave said, "You fell. What happened there?"

Was he trying to change the subject? "I didn't see a rock and I tripped."

"Then?" Dave waited.

"I started watching you more carefully. I saw where you

were stepping and followed your foot placements. Do you realize you tap twice on rocks and roots that are potential tripping hazards? It's like you were communicating to me without . . ." I stopped. I was hungry earlier, but I didn't realize I would be eating crow now. . . "saying a word" I finished.

I looked up to see Dave's eyebrow lifted in knowing curiosity.

I continued, "You were communicating. Just without words. Wow, I feel like a jerk. I'm sorry for blowing up at you." The Jedi was teaching the padawan.

"Apology accepted. Now let's talk about that word. Communication. What are some ways we can communicate?"

The question hung for a second as I thought, "well obviously we can communicate without words."

"Good," Dave replied. "So non-verbal communication. What other ways?"

"Like we are right now. *Using words.*" I emphasized the last part. The tension had broken, and I laughed.

Laughing with me Dave said, "Verbal. Nice. Any other ways?" His eyes moved to the notebook he had given me. A welcomed hint.

"Written communication." I said.

"Very good Paul. As a leader, communicating is one of

the most vital things you need to work on and be proficient in. Communication comes in three basic forms. Verbal, non-verbal, and written. Answer this as quick as you can. Who was the best communicator you ever met?"

It didn't take me long, "My high school drama teacher."

"Great. Now what made them the best?"

"He had a way of making difficult concepts easy to understand." I thought some more. "I remember vividly when he wanted to really get our attention with something, he would almost talk in a whisper very slowly. Oh! He was also notorious hand talker as well. You should have seen him get excited and wave his hands like a mad man. We used to call him the human helicopter because it felt like at any moment he was going to fly away." I smiled at the memory.

"Fantastic Paul. So, what I heard you say is that your teacher used pace and tone in his verbal communication and emphasized with his hands for non-verbal communication?"

"Well. . . yea I guess." I hadn't thought of it broken out like that. It all just made sense when it was happening.

"It must have had an impact on you because he is the first person to come to mind. Pace and tone are two important parts of verbal communication. Used effectively, they can create suspense, draw people in, like you said, or add seriousness to a statement. If I said to you, 'have a nice day' in a tone that was light and jumpy what would you think?"

"I would think that you want me to have a nice day" I laughed.

Dave continued, "now imagine I say 'have a nice day' in a short and monotone voice. Would you still believe that I want you to have a nice day?"

"No" I replied. "I would think you want me to go away or you are upset at me."

"But they are the same words Paul. Shouldn't they mean the same thing?"

Cue the lightbulb. "I see what you mean. There are tons of ways to say one thing. Pace and tone help distinguish. Could adding a pointed finger toward the door could be non-verbal way to communicate after that last one?"

"Exactly!" Dave was excited that I was catching on. "Now if I waved at you like I was saying a friendly goodbye and had a smile on my face, while at the same time gave you the short monotone have a nice day, that would be weird right?"

"Very" I said. "I might think you were a robot."

"Have you ever seen a leader give a presentation on something they should be excited about, but their arms were crossed, and they looked down most of the time? What does that communicate?"

"That they aren't as excited as they should be," I said.

"I would think the same thing," said Dave. "You would be surprised how many people actually do that. I think you get the idea of verbal and non-verbal, but what have we left out?"

"Written," I answered.

"Ah the joys of written communication," Dave said. "Why do you think I gave you that journal?"

"Is this a trick question?" I smiled. "To write in."

"Yes, to write in." Dave smiled too. "What do you plan to write in it?"

I thought for a moment. "Well I will probably write about the trip so far. Maybe some thoughts on what we have talked about and some of my feelings leading up to this trip."

"Great!" Dave said, then his smile faded. "Now what if I told you that whatever you write is going to be read by everyone at the office, including those who you are about to lead?"

I panicked a bit. "Whoa, is that really what's going to happen? In that case I would probably leave out my personal thoughts and probably just write some notes on leadership. Keep it simple and brief. Is that really what it is for? I mean, I'm fine with that if it is, but . . ."

Dave interrupted me with a laugh, "No." He looked at

his notebook. "But you need to remember that with any written communication, once it is out there . . .it is out there. With scanners, phone cameras and the ease of forwarding emails, any written communication can be shared almost immediately and indefinitely. It can help you or hurt you."

I thought for a moment. It had never occurred to me that what I write could be shared so quickly. I guess it is because I grew up in that world.

Dave went on, "I personally have found written communication to be one of the hardest communications of all. Why do you think that is?"

"Well, sometimes people can read something differently than you intended when you wrote it. I had a girlfriend in high school that broke up with me because I texted her "I'm with my friends." I shook my head at the memory and laughed. "The craziest part is *she* asked me what I was doing! I was answering the question, and she read it as if I had typed 'leave me alone because I don't want to be with you ever again'. Can you imagine?"

"Yes I can" Dave said knowingly. "One of the biggest hurdles of written communication is that it lacks what verbal communication has ---- pace, tone and non-verbal cues. That is why it is vitally important to keep written communication short, concise and appropriate. If you don't feel it will land how you want, then you should probably deliver it in person."

My head was spinning a bit with all these ideas. Dave saw the wheels turning and graciously relented, "Well, that's enough for now Paul. I'm going to turn in for the night. Hang out by the fire as long as you want but do me a favor and add a log or two before you go to bed so I don't have to re-light it in the morning." With that he headed to the tent.

I nodded in recognition and pulled the pen out of the spine of my notebook. I needed to put these things in writing. I paused briefly, slightly wondering if Dave really was going to share my journal entry. Then another lightbulb moment hit me: This is the way I should feel whenever I write any kind of communication. "Well done Jedi Dave" I thought to myself and smiled.

Communication Types

1. Verbal
    a. Two factors:
        i. Pace - rate of speed
        ii. Tone - pitch and inflection
2. Non-Verbal
    a. Make sure the actions match the message
    b. Danger: Can be a distraction more than an addition (the helicopter)
3. Written
    a. Write as if it lasts forever and can be shared instantly
    b. Be short, concise and appropriate
    c. If you don't feel it will communicate well in written, communicate in person
    d. Danger: No pace and tone

CHAPTER 6

TERROR

I awoke to the light of the morning sun and the sounds of birds chirping. "That's a first," I thought. I looked over to find an empty sleeping bag where Dave was supposed to be sleeping. Either I was too exhausted to wake up, or Dave had some crazy Ninja skills that I didn't account for in his skill set.

My body felt like I had superglued my joints together. As I unzipped the tent, I saw that Dave was by the fire with breakfast almost done.

"Early bird huh?" I said in a groggy voice.

"You know, I never could sleep in that late when I'm in the woods. I guess I'm afraid I'm going to miss something."

I took a moment to stretch my arms and legs, hoping to subdue the pain a bit.

Dave smiled and said, "I always found it helpful to do

some jumping jacks or run in place. Works out the stiffness."

He was right. After a few minutes of both exercises, I felt way better. After a quick breakfast of re-hydrated something and pumping some water through the filter into our water bottles, we sat down to look at the map.

"Alright Paul, here is where we are." He pointed to a location on the map. "Today we are going to work our way through this part of the trail and try to camp here." As his finger followed the path across the page, I stopped listening and my eyes got locked on a feature Dave seemed to have glazed over.

"Dave!"

"Paul?" Dave stopped and looked up.

"If my limited map reading abilities are correct, this thin blue line represents a river."

"You got it," He said in a happy go lucky tone. He drew his finger across the map again from where we were to where we were headed, and it happened again. His finger went right over the blue line like it was nothing but a puddle.

"So we are crossing a river? Like an actual moving body of water with current and rapids and. . ." I trailed off.

Dave replied, "Yes." It wasn't a question like 'is that a problem.' It was just a simple fact and the deal was done. "We won't know until we get there if it is shallow enough to just walk across or if the rains last week mean we will have to wade across."

Now anyone who played Oregon Trail as a kid knows, if you ford the river . . . it is always a gamble that you will lose everything. Little Johnny might come down with pneumonia, your oxen drown, and game is over!

Dave must have seen the fear. "Paul, can you put your trust in me to get us across safely?"

All I could do was nod. I did trust Dave, but the question was. . . did I trust him enough?

It took about twenty minutes to break down camp and pack up our backpacks. After everything was put away, Dave went around our campsite with a fallen tree branch and, I can't make this stuff up, he swept the ground. After that, he poured 4 pots filled with water on the campfire, stirred around the extinguished coals with a stick, and threw the rocks in all different directions. Now to me this seemed like the actions of a crazy man, but Dave was moving through it like it was just another part of his morning routine.

My pack was slightly less awkward after wearing it yesterday. I no longer felt like Luke Skywalker with Yoda on my back, the bad news was. . . well, in a few short miles we were going to cross a river.

"You ready to roll?" Dave said.

"As I'll ever be." I was not ready, but I was going.

The trail to the river was quite easy. Since rivers are just low points between elevation on each side, the trail was mostly downhill. The terrified voice in my head was the hard part. I kept wondering what was about to happen. Then my mind went to the wrong place. I recalled my earlier Google search. Did I read about anyone drowning? Did I call my parents before I left? I should have listened to my financial guy and bought life insurance. Who will feed Bruce, my betta fish? That is the one that brought me back to reality. I tried to focus on the trail and Dave's foot placement, but it wasn't long before the sound of water grew louder. With each step my nerves were starting to show.

"Dave, is there a trail that doesn't require us to cross the river?"

"Yea!" Dave stopped and turned around. Sweet relief flooded over me. He pointed behind me with his best smile, "that one." Relief gone.

"Oh" I managed to get out.

The trail narrowed and became steep toward the bank. There it was, my fear in fluid motion. In front of us, the river was gracefully flowing from left to right. The sun was hitting it perfectly, and the water was so clear you could see the rocks below. It suddenly reminded me of the scene on some of the bottles of water you purchase at the gas station. If it were not for the knowledge that I was about to cross this flowing death trap, it would have been a very peaceful place.

Dave went into a serious mood. His eyes were focused, and I could tell that he was taking charge. It was comforting to have him fully engaged, and I certainly was all ears. Drowning was not part of my plan for today.

"Paul, I'm going to walk you through every step of this. We are going to talk about what is going to happen, practice on land, and then we are going to do it." I nodded.

"Let's take a look at this water shall we?" We walked to the shoreline, and Dave looked to his left and right. Due to the sound of the water, Dave spoke at a little less than a shout. "When you are crossing a moving body of water, you want to account for a couple things. First, find the widest spot. This is where the water will be the shallowest." He pointed to a stretch of the river, about 20 steps upstream. "Once you find that, you want to look as far down river as you can. You are looking for any hazards that could be dangerous should you decide to take a dip." He smiled. I did not. "Now ideally, you don't want to cross at a place that is higher than your knees and never one that is higher than your waist." I was just about to ask how you figure that out when he picked up a rock and threw it at the middle of the river. It gave a lighter splash, and the ripples were quickly overcome by the current.

"Did you hear that?" Dave asked.

"Yea" I said blankly, wondering where this was going.

"Now listen to this one." Dave moved 10 steps upriver where it narrowed and threw another softball size rock. *Kerplunk.* The sound was deep and resonating. "That is the sound of deep water." I could tell Dave knew his stuff, but head knowledge is one thing, action is something totally different.

Dave went on, "We are going to unbuckle our packs but keep them on our shoulders. If you feel like you are about to fall in or are losing your balance, better to have a wet pack down river than risk a water rescue." Well at least that made sense. I briefly daydreamed of just throwing the pack in the river before stepping foot in the water, but quickly decided that probably wasn't the smartest move.

"We are going to link arms and shuffle sideways across. You will be beside me, and I will be the first to enter the water. In our arms that aren't linked together, we will have one of the hiking poles for added stability." I hadn't even thought of that. His focus was causing me to focus as well. With that, my mind was starting to ease with each detail of Dave's instruction.

"Did you pack water shoes?" Dave asked.

"Was it on the checklist?"

"Yep"

"Then I packed it." After all, I was an engineer. Details are kind of our thing.

"Good. We have another 4 miles after this, and it would be a nightmare to do it in wet boots and socks. How about we get some practice in?" He set down his pack and started to unlace his boots. After a quick footwear change, we were once again standing on the shore with our packs on. Dave judged a length of the rocky shoreline that matched the width of the river crossing.

"Now we are going to shuffle sideways, but I only want you to look forward. The water will refract light when we cross for real, so you really won't be able to judge your footsteps at the bottom. We want to practice like the real thing."

With my pole in hand, the river behind me and Dave on my right, we shuffled our way across the shore. I found myself extremely tempted to look down. It is one of those things you don't really think about until you are told you can't do it. My foot hit a larger rock, and I strained my concentration to keep from looking at what was blocking my path.

I asked Dave, "Can we pause for a second?" I had an idea that would make it easier for me. "Dave, do you think you could call out what you are walking on so I could be prepared before I get to it?"

"Absolutely! Great idea! Wait, have you done this before?" He gave a sly smile.

Dave calling out what he was experiencing was actually way more helpful than I originally thought. We finished the dry run, pun intended, without much incident and made our way back to the crossing section. It was time to face the giant.

CHAPTER 7

TRUST AND DELEGATION

The river was beautiful and the birds were singing, but all I could hear was my heart racing. As an engineer, my focus has always been on process, details, and double checking my work. There was no double checking in this scenario. I was as prepared as I would be, and it was go time.

Dave stepped first into the water. After his foot was engulfed by water, he laughed, "Wow that's cold!" He stepped out further as I took my first step in the water, and I found out that he was not lying. My mind registered the temperature for a millisecond before returning to my adrenaline filled focus. Unhurriedly, we shuffled step by step. Dave was a man of his word and called out what he was experiencing so I could be prepared. The water climbed higher on my leg with every tedious step. We had made it to the middle of the crossing and then ------ fear struck me.

"I'm slipping!" I cried out. My mind went into overdrive. Should I drop my pack? Dave's reaction was instantaneous. He tightened his shoulder muscles and planted his pole. My body went into autopilot. I felt his arm lock, and I leaned hard on it. My foot that was slipping found secure footing in a gap between two rocks, and we both stood still as statues.

"You okay Paul?"

"Yea. You?" My voice unsurprisingly strained.

"I am." Dave replied with a steady tone. "Ready to take the next step?"

I nodded and we gradually moved on.

Thanks to Dave's instructions and surprisingly strong shoulder muscles, we completed the crossing and took our first steps on dry land.

To use the word 'elated' would be an understatement. Adrenaline, fear, joy, doubt, courage, gratefulness and pride exploded out of me at once. I couldn't help what happened next. I turned around to face my enemy. With arms stretched wide, I yelled at the top of my lungs from somewhere deep inside me. I surprised myself with the volume. If felt like nothing short of an all-out roar. As the last of my breath left my lungs, I was surprised to find that the sound continued. At first, I thought there was an echo across the water, but as I looked to my left, I saw Dave standing beside me, arms stretched wide, roaring with all that he had at the flowing foe that had been vanquished. A slight grin on his face as he did so. The remaining four miles of the hike were a blur, but the smile on my face was constant. I had conquered the unthinkable. Well, at least unthinkable in my mind. My steps felt lighter, and I even set up the tent at our next campsite on the first attempt. What a glorious day!

The rehydrated dinner around the campfire was filled with laughter, and every detail of the monumental event. Dave recounted his reaction to my all-out terror moment in the middle of the river. In turn gave him the play by play of my thoughts, including multiple four-letter words that I had managed to keep internalized in the moment.

Dave finished his pouch of chicken and dumplings and added another log to the fire.

"Paul, I'm so proud of what you accomplished today." Dave said smiling from ear to ear.

"Well I could not have done it without you." I meant it. "Honestly, if you had asked me how I would cross a river one week ago, I would have politely answered 'on the nearest bridge'."

We both laughed. As he stuffed the pouch in the Ziplock bag Dave said, "I would like to talk to you about another element of leadership."

I had been looking forward to this since the river crossing and was genuinely excited to hear Dave's insights.

"What do you think of when you hear the word 'trust'?" he asked.

I thought for a moment. "I think of summer camp."

Dave laughed. "Okay. Not what I thought you would say but go on."

"My cabin did this activity on a challenge course called the blind walk." Dave smiled and nodded indicating he was familiar with it. "Each person had to take a turn walking on a plank that started on the ground but ended at an elevation. Your cabin mates were supposed to guide you step by step and catch you if you fall. It was terrifying at the time. You had to have some sliver of trust that your group would guide you well and if you did fall, that you would not be met by the hard ground."

"That is a great exercise of trust" Dave acknowledged. "I especially like your description that there had to be some element of trust before action was taken. Did they catch you?"

"No" I blurted out in laughter and Dave wasn't far behind.

"Wait, they let you hit the ground?" I had his full attention.

"No . . . I never did it. The counselor gave us the option

to opt out before we started, and I took it." I said.

"I see" Dave nodded. "Do you regret it?"

"Yes . . . I always wondered what it would have been like. I decided I would do it next time but that was the only summer I went to camp, and I lost my only opportunity."

Dave pointed out, "You lost the opportunity for that event, but you showed tremendous trust today at the river. I would argue more trust than a four-foot fall to the ground would need."

"I can't argue with you there." I replied.

"Trust is one of the hardest things to give. In the area of leadership, it is not only vital that we give it, but also vital that we receive it." I was surprised by that second part, but it made sense.

I asked, "So I have heard a lot about giving trust, but I am interested that getting it is just as important."

"It is!" Dave replied. "Look at both through the lens of our adventure today. Where did you see the elements of gaining trust?"

This wasn't too difficult for me. "From the moment I found out we were crossing a river; I was very distrusting. It was not a lack of trust in you though." I wanted Dave to understand I wasn't doubting him. "If I really think about it, I was lacking in trust of my own ability. In terms of gaining trust, you did some things that built my trust. First off, you have been really knowledgeable throughout this trip so far so I felt you knew what you were doing and would have a plan. Second, you were so confident and calm. It was freaky at first, but then I realized it was creating a sense of calmness and confidence in me as well. You told me exactly what was going to happen and why. At that point I was honestly not going to do it, but what you did next pushed me to take my first step in the water. We practiced on the shoreline. Man, I cannot tell you what that did for me."

"Those are great observations about gaining trust." Dave said. "And in leadership, they all have application for your people. Showing confidence in yourself and in your people. Communicating what to expect before it happens. Giving people examples and a safe place to make mistakes. All of those things help you gain trust."

Dave went on, "I'll tell you what I saw about you in the area of giving trust. You mentioned that you weren't going to do it until a certain point. You had some trust in me, but not enough to take action. It is important to remember that trust is like a bank account. Depending on the withdrawal, you need to have enough in the bank account."

"Or your payment will be denied" I interjected.

"Well said." Dave laughed. "When you took the first step into the water, you put action to your trust. You didn't have 100% trust at that point, but you had enough to act.

You also displayed a massive amount of trust when you slipped. You could have dumped your pack and tried to balance on your own, but instead you leaned on me for support. You trusted me with your balance and safety."

"Can we talk about your freakish dad strength?" I laughed.

Dave laughed for a moment, and then with a deadpan expression said, "no." We both exploded in laughter. After calming down, Dave continued.

"Now let's talk about trust in action. For leaders, one of the main ways to do this through delegation."

"Oh yea, like when you give me your work so you can sit in your office and watch Netflix." I said, hoping it would get a rise out of Dave.

"Exactly! I couldn't have finished the final season of 'The Office' without you." Dave was quick. No doubt about it.

Dave reoriented the conversation, "In reality, delegation is trust. Let me ask you, who do you think hears about it, good or bad, when the work gets turned in?"

"You do." I said.

"So, in reality, I have trusted you with my reputation."

I thought for a moment. "I'm a little ashamed to say that I never looked at it that way."

Dave continued. "At the river, I purposefully followed

four key steps: 1) I own it, 2) you see it, 3) you do it, 4) you take it. For each one of those steps, I play a different role. I owned the river crossing far before we ever planned this trip. I have done hundreds of them, even some by myself. When I'm by myself, I don't have to trust you at all, and I simply rely on my own ability. I am the sole facilitator of the event. Now when you enter the picture, I need to move to the stage where 'you see it'. I described exactly what was going to happen and how it would happen for a reason. I outlined the steps that would take place and what you needed to consider before crossing a river. I was the guide. I was moving you through. Does this make sense so far?"

"Yes." I had pulled out my notebook because this was far more than I could hold in my head.

Dave then said, "Then came time to practice. At that point we moved to the 'you do it' stage. You participated in the activity. You gained clarity around what it would be like in a safe environment before we did it together for real. You had a great idea while we were practicing, do you remember it?"

"I asked if you could describe what was ahead so I could be more prepared." I said proudly.

"That was so great! You thought of something that I hadn't considered to make the event better. After we practiced, we crossed the river side by side. It is important to note that we did it together. I didn't just leave you to it and hope for the best. When you slipped, I was there with my, 'dad strength' as you call it, to lean on. At that stage I was the mentor. Someone with experience to walk *with* you... or in our case shuffle." Dave smiled. "The final stage, you do it, is one that we haven't achieved yet. When you take full ownership of crossing a river without my help, the full cycle of delegation will be complete."

"I don't know if I'm there yet." I said, wondering if there were more rivers in our future.

"I don't know if you are either." Dave chuckled. "But at that stage, I would be the empowerer, relinquishing all control ----- aka trust," Dave winked. "for you to lead moving forward."

I finished the notes I had made and looked up, ready for more. Dave stretched and yawned. "Welp, I think I am going to call it a night. Would you mind . . ."

"Putting another log on the fire before I head in." I interrupted. Dave nodded in approval and headed to the tent. My notes looked like frantic chicken scratch, so I took a few minutes to consolidate them.

Trust and Delegation

2 Elements of Trust

1. Getting Trust

    a. Showing confidence in myself and confidence in my people helps build trust.

    b. Communicating expectations

    c. Allowing people to make mistakes and give input

2. Giving Trust

    a. Trust Bank Account - People might have a percentage of trust in you, but that amount will depend on their action which is a withdraw.

    b. Trust is given in many ways, but a big one in work is delegation

Delegation

I Own It

    1.   I have all the control and trust only myself.

    2.   Role: Facilitator

You see it

    1.   As the leader, I give a detailed explanation of what the task is.

    2.   Trust is given in a small way.

    3.   Role: Guide

You Do It

    1.   As the leader, I stand alongside someone as they do the task

    2.   Practice

    3.   Trust is given and gained by completing the task well

    4.   Role: Mentor

You take it

    1.   I as the leader have passed the baton

    2.   Be available but not alongside

    3.   Trust is close to, or fully, given

    4.   Role: Empowerer

CHAPTER 8

VALUES

I was getting the hang of this backpacking thing. The morning ran as smooth as it could. I actually heard Dave leave the tent and remembered his words, "I guess I feel like I'm going to miss out on something." It must have been enough to pique my curiosity because I couldn't go back to sleep. After ten minutes of tossing and turning, I finally gave up and decided to start the day.

I unzipped the tent and saw Dave blowing on the fire to ignite a fresh set of wood. I was surprised to find two coffee cups steaming with that dark drink of the gods next to our fire. I thought to myself, "how did he know I was . . . oh wait! Jedi." I am not much of a plain coffee guy, but I had a surprise up my sleeve. I retrieved a dry packet of hot chocolate from my pack and walked back to gloat in my wisdom.

Dave looked surprised as I poured half the packet in one of the cups. I held the remainder of the packet in Dave's direction with raised eyebrows to see if he was interested. He motioned with his palm up toward his cup as if to say, "by all means." After a quick stir with a nearby twig, our mochas were served.

"You've done this before?" Dave asked.

"Googled it."

With a slow nod and a smile, Dave returned to the silence of the early morning sunrise. . . and what a sunrise it was.

Dave pulled out the map after finishing his coffee, and I caught another look at his warn, gold, compass. If that compass could talk, I'm sure it would have some amazing stories to tell. After a quick look and tracing the trail with his finger, Dave folded the map and put the compass away. I was more than relieved to see that there were no blue lines in our path today.

After a quiet breakfast of biscuits and gravy, rehydrated of course, Dave was the first to break the silence. "You ready to pack up?"

"Yep"

We both started the process with relative efficiency. We each rolled and packed our sleeping bags and sleeping pads, broke down the tent, and separated the parts into each backpack to divide the load. When everything was all but packed away, once again, Dave poured a large amount of water onto the fire and held his hand above it to feel for remaining coals. After he felt it was sufficiently out, he went about throwing the rocks in different directions and spreading around the water-soaked coals with a stick. I watched in curiosity. I knew what was coming next, but I still couldn't believe it was actually happening. Dave took a large fallen branch and swept it around the site. He literally swept the dirt.

This time I could not hold my tongue. "Dave . . . what on earth are you doing?"

Dave finished his ceremonial task and leaned against the branch like a crutch.

"I was wondering when you were going to ask. I'm sweeping." Dave smiled. "Have you ever heard of 'Leave No Trace' principles?"

"I haven't, but the name gives it away a bit."

"That it does. Tell me Paul, what did you think of this campsite when we arrived?"

"I thought it looked like we were the first people on earth to use it."

"Take a few steps back." Dave said as he pointed with the makeshift broom.

I walked back a few steps and turned around. "Okay."

"What does it look like now?"

"Other than our packs leaning on the tree it looks like we were never here."

"Exactly, we left . . ."

"No trace." I finished for him.

"I've been backpacking a couple of times," Dave smirked. "The principles of 'Leave No Trace' are no longer just principles for me. They are part of my values on the trail."

I nodded in understanding, still not quite sure if that was a logical explanation for his behavior.

"Let's talk more about values while we hike. Today is the long leg and we're burning daylight."

Putting on my hiking boots this morning should have been my first warning that I was going to pay for not breaking them in like Dave suggested. I could feel the spots where the skin was sensitive as I slipped each shoe over my feet. I was relieved that after the first few steps, they began to settle in for the long hike ahead.

It didn't take long for Dave to circle back to our conversation on values. I could tell it was on his mind, and this is something he had been wanting to share with me. I was just as eager to learn.

"So, what is one of your core values Paul?" Dave said as he tapped twice on a protruding root.

Truthfully, I hadn't really put much thought into that particular subject. I replied with the first thing that came to mind, "honesty."

"That's a fantastic moral. What is one of your values?"

I was confused. "What do you mean? Isn't honesty a value?"

"Honesty itself is not a value. Now, if you said, 'to do the right thing,' that would be a value and inside of that might contain some morals, like honesty. Let me go a step further in describing this. Another word for moral is ethical. It is a choice of right and wrong. If you are not honest, you are not being ethical. Values, on the other hand, are the guiding principles that you live your life on. If I told you one of my values is timeliness, that would demonstrate itself by quickly responding to emails or being on time, or even early, for meetings. If I constantly show up late, you would not say that I am unethical or immoral. I simply don't have a value of timeliness. See the difference?"

"I think so."

"Here's another example. If you work with someone who is always guarded, you might feel frustrated at their coldness, maybe even feel that you don't trust them. In reality, they might simply have a value of extreme professionalism, while you value openness."

"Okay. I think I get it."

"So how do you think this relates to leadership?"

I took a moment to mostly to gather my thoughts, but also to catch my breath because we had just finished a pretty steep section of the trail. "You said values are the guiding principles that you live your life by . . . I would assume you need to have core values that you lead by as well?"

"Well said Paul! You are right on the money. A great leader knows and leads from their values. It is the compass of their leadership." He stopped and reached in his pocket and pulled out his compass. "This compass is a powerful tool out here. One of the most important things it does is orients the map. A map is a useful tool as well, but without knowing where North is, the map can only tell us so much. If we were out here with no trail to follow, we would have to find landmarks that match the map----like that mountain peak over there." He pointed slightly to the left at a pinnacle in the distance.

"Between here and there is a lot of terrain. If we walked through a thick forest, we would lose sight of the peak, but if we use the compass and set a bearing to the peak, we can follow that bearing through any thicket or forest and still make it to our desired destination. That is what a leader's values do."

"But what if you get off course?" I asked.

"Oh man. That is where it can get hairy. One of the dangers of using the compass is forgetting to look down at it often. The further out the target, the more risk that you can get off course. Even the slightest degree in error could put you in dangerous territory. So, for a leader, it is vital to continually reorient to their values to make sure they are on course. Without them, you could very easily end up somewhere you never intended to be."

Dave put the compass back in his pocket and motioned for me to take the lead on the trail. Without the task of concentrating on Dave's backside and his non-verbal communication in front of me, I had time to let the concepts Dave talked about sink in. I mentally compiled my thoughts for my journal entry. There was only one thing keeping me from complete concentration . . . my feet were beginning to hurt.

Values

1. Values are not morals.

   a. You can have morals inside of a value, but they are not values by themselves.

2. Values are the guiding principles that a leader leads with.

3. Values are like a compass

   a. They should be checked often to keep from going astray.

   b. Can be used to show the way when the end goal is not in your immediate vision.

   c. Without them you could end up somewhere you never intended to be.

CHAPTER 9

PAIN

I could feel Dave walking closer behind me. I knew why too. I was slowing down. Every time I felt him getting closer, I knew I had to pick up the pace. I doubled down on my resolve and pushed myself harder and harder. Luckily Dave could not see my tormented face as each step unraveled my new reality---pain.

My right heel felt like it was being stung by a thousand ants with every step. Sadly, that would be considered my good foot. My left heel felt the same but with an additional searing pain near my pinky toe. To make matters worse, we just started a particularly hard section of the trail on a decline. Most people think going downhill is easy, but in this case, it was the most excruciating part.

I tried everything to lessen the pain. I tried walking on my toes, but that made me want to cut my left foot off and throw it in the woods. I tried walking flat footed, but somehow that aggravated both feet. I found a slight bit of relief waddling like a duck with my feet pointed out, but I felt like an idiot with Dave behind me so that didn't last long.

I was now in full blown regret for not breaking in my new boots. I secretly knew what Dave meant by 'wear them before we started,' but I didn't feel like it was that big of a deal. It is now a BIG DEAL.

My mind simply could not cover up the pain. I tried everything. I started reciting poems in my head. That eventually morphed into singing songs. One that seemed particularly fitting was' The Sound of Silence' by Simon and Garfunkel. "Hello darkness my old friend, I've come to talk with you again" on repeat over and over in my head!

I could feel Dave edging closer. My thoughts were filled with the nerves sending pain signals to my brain and the growing anger at Dave's continued oppression. I know I was slower than him, but did he have to draft me like a Nascar driver! Step. Pain. Step. Pain. I couldn't take it anymore.

"That's it!" I shouted and took my last step.

"What's it?"

I threw off my pack and it landed with a thud. "Do you

really have to follow me so closely? Any closer and I would be carrying you as well."

"Paul, what's wrong?"

My volcano of anger quickly subsided when I realized Dave was expressing genuine concern for me. My anger was replaced by guilt at my harsh tone. I took a deep breath to calm down. I did this to myself. "I'm sorry. It is not your fault." I couldn't look him in the eye.

"Your feet are in bad shape aren't they." Dave said compassionately.

"Bad is an understatement."

"Sit down and take your boots and socks off. Let's see what we are working with."

Sitting down brought a beautiful moment of sweet relief. As I took my boots off, a strong indicator of the problem was the red stain mark on my left sock. I delicately removed the final layer of socks and could see the full state of my condition. My right heel was cherry red with a blister the size of a quarter protruding from it. My left heel bore a similar fate, with the worst of it on my pinky toe. I was in rough shape

"Ouch!" was all Dave could manage as he kneeled down. "Lift your feet up." I did as instructed. Dave was careful not to aggravate any of the wounds. After a quick assessment, he dropped his pack and started to unzip the front compartment. He pulled out a Ziplock bag with what looked like large puffy Band-Aids neatly flattened in a row.

"Okay. These are going to help our problem, but they come with a price."

"A price?" I said with an upward inflection.

"The glue that keeps these adhered to your skin is very strong. They cover the blisters, but pulling them off is going to feel like I am lighting your skin on fire." I winced at the thought.

"If it will help now, I can worry about that later. I'm going to look away while you pop them."

"I'm not going to."

"Wait! Why not?"

"Your body has done what it has done for a reason. The blister is filled with fluid which is a barrier protecting the skin from the nerve receptors."

"In that case . . . don't pop them."

Dave went to work. He made short order of the repair. Both heels received a large patch, and the side of my left foot received two. After a brief inspection of his work, Dave put the Ziplock away and retrieved a thin pair of socks from his pack.

"Do you have another pair of socks? Dry socks make happy feet." I nodded and rummaged through my pack. "Put these on before your new pair. They are thinner and will act as fake skin."

"Thanks. I'll get them back to you."

"Uuuhhhhh, they are yours now." The look of disgust on Dave's face made me burst out in laughter.

I carefully put the thin socks on followed by the dry pair. My feet felt bulky but at the same time protected. Dave suggested we take an early lunch to let my feet relax, and I relished the idea.

When you're hungry, everything tastes good. In this case it was tuna packets with ranch and crackers. "I'm going to stock my apartment with these when I get home." I said with half a cracker still in my mouth.

Dave laughed and said, "I thought that too when I had my first few on the trail. The interesting thing is, it tastes different at home . . . in a not so great way."

"Interesting," I thought. Dave's knowledge so far had proven to be on point, so I reconsidered my bulk Costco order. "Any leadership words of wisdom from all this?" I said, motioning toward my feet and boots.

"Actually . . . yes." Dave seemed pleased that I asked.

"This should be good. Let me guess, we have already talked about preparation so that isn't it. Maybe listening to wise counsel? Or wait . . . I have it. . . rubbing people the wrong way!"

Dave smiled, "I think you are on to something there,

but I was thinking more about the area of feedback."

"Feedback . . . I'm intrigued. Go on." The food was definitely lifting my spirits.

"How about you start. Why did you wait until the last possible moment to let me know your problem?"

I didn't see that coming, but I knew I deserved it. "I guess I wanted to power through. On some level, I didn't want to be the squeaky wheel. Probably a bit of pride mixed in there too."

"I see." Dave seemed pleased with my vulnerability. "Feedback is like a two-lane road, and you are standing in the middle. On one side, you have feedback moving away from you. That would be giving feedback. On the other side, you have feedback moving towards you, getting feedback." I reached into my pack to retrieve my notebook because I liked where this was going.

Dave paused to let me get ready, then continued. "For most leaders, one lane is easier than another. Some have no problem giving feedback, but struggle with receiving it. Others welcome feedback but cannot see the value in giving it. Continuing with the road analogy, a two-lane road is built for both ways. If the cars only move in one direction, there is a problem."

"Yea, like construction or an accident."

"Precisely! In both of those scenarios, there is someone

who is frustrated. If a leader has a problem giving feedback, their people will be left with no guidance or direction. In some cases, like our situation earlier," Dave raised his eyebrows and smiled from the corner of his mouth, "the leader can store up feedback and then open the floodgates on their people. Most of the time people get hurt or think, 'why didn't you say something sooner?'"

"Yea . . sorry about that."

Dave waved his hand dismissively, "It helped anchor the concept for you, did it not?"

I looked up from my notes, "Yea, I would rather avoid anchoring anything in the future."

Dave continued, "I have found over the years that giving feedback has five essential steps to make it as effective as possible. First, make it timely. Not to rub salt on the wound," Dave smiled at his pun, "but if you had not waited so long to give your feedback, you could have avoided a lot of pain. Second, you need to ask permission. I like to ask, 'is now an okay time to talk about some things?'" The reason why you do this is because you don't know what is going on in the other person's life. They could be having the worst day, and it has reflected itself in their actions. Third, you need to come at it with curiosity, not making accusations. This does two things. It is much easier to hear from their perspective, *and* it is much easier to ask from your perspective. Fourth, you need to give concrete examples. Nothing is more confusing than vague feedback like, 'do better,' or 'this was not your best work'. When you give examples, it gives clarity to what went right or wrong and gives people a way to fix it. Without concrete examples, people are simply frustrated. Finally, after the feedback is given, you need to listen. Your people might have legitimate reasons for their actions that you had not accounted for, but if you end the conversation, it can leave people to feel dejected and frustrated."

As I finished writing down the five points of giving feedback, I smiled in recognition that Dave had used this very framework on me.

"You've done that with me before. Honestly, it didn't even feel like feedback."

"When you do it well, it won't. Now, it is important that you consistently give both constructive and positive feedback. If you lean heavily to one side or the other, it can lead to tough times."

"I get that." I said. "I had a former boss who only gave positive feedback. It was great, don't get me wrong, but when he gave me constructive feedback for the first time, I thought I was about to get fired!"

"Like I said, I have learned over this time. Mostly from doing it wrong. But that is a good segway into the other lane, receiving feedback." I prepped my pen and paper.

"When it comes to anxiety about feedback, a lot of it has to do with receiving it. Because not everyone is great at giving it, a good leader should be prepared to receive feedback in a healthy way, no matter what the form, and the feedback should not shatter your world. It helps to remember that we receive feedback all the time and don't realize it. Anything from car horns to a dog's tail wagging. Our mind takes the feedback, processes it, and adjusts accordingly. All we need to do is keep that same mindset. Make sense?"

It did. I nodded as I wrote. My feet were thankful that there was more.

"So, there are three basic things you need to do to receive feedback in a healthy way. First, you need to listen intently. Note here I used the word 'listen' for a reason. We can hear the rain. You can *hear* your mom tell you a story, but that is just an acknowledgement that sounds are being received by your brain. When you listen, those sounds get digested and your brain works to organize them into logical thought. This requires some work on your part. Before receiving feedback, you need to be aware of your time and brainpower. If you don't have enough of one or the other, then you need to politely move the feedback to another time."

"How do you do that without offending someone?"

"Tell them the truth." Dave shifted his weight and looked directly at me. "Paul, at this current time I can't give you the full attention that you deserve, and I want to give it to you! Do you think we could have this conversation to a later time today or maybe tomorrow?" Dave said it with such sincerity that I almost forgot he was role playing.

"Got it. I should make sure I am able to do the work of listening."

"The second thing you need to do comes after they are finished with the feedback. Because you have listened intently, you can then repeat back the points of their feedback in your own words. This is called 'framing'. There is beauty in this. If you are right on with your framing, you gain clarity and the person who gave you the feedback feels heard and respected. If you are incorrect, then they will clarify it correctly for you, and again, they feel heard and respected."

"So really, it has no downside."

"It really doesn't! That brings us to the third and final thing you need to do-- thank them for their feedback and end the conversation. I know what you are thinking, if you end the conversation, you can't reply back to them." I was thinking that. "The thing is Paul, thanking and ending the conversation is the safest thing. When you thank them, you are showing them that you are open to feedback, and when you leave, you prevent saying something you will possibly regret in the heat of the moment. The conversation doesn't have to end completely, it just needs to end for now."

I must have had a look on my face because Dave didn't continue. I asked "But what if they ask you for your thoughts? Like they are looking for a response?"

"That can, and will, happen. I found the phrase, 'I need some time to digest what we talked about' works every time."

"I think I'm going to need some time to digest all this knowledge on feedback right now," I said jokingly but was really serious.

"I know it is a lot, but I have one more important thing for you when getting feedback. While you need to listen intently, which we talked about, you must address the behavior. If you always take the feedback but never change . . . your people will stop giving it." I underlined that final thought.

"That's enough for now." Dave slapped his knee before standing up. "Finish digesting, I'll take a look at the map and see what distance we have left for today." Dave opened the map just as a gust of wind blew past. Dave managed to hold on to the paper, but he looked up at the sky for a long time afterward. Smiling he said, "Fun . . . it looks like rain."

Feedback

1. 5 steps to giving feedback
   a. Make it timely - don't wait too long
   b. Ask Permission - if not now, when
   c. Come at it curious - you don't know what is going on yet
   d. Be Specific - Use concrete examples
   e. Listen - only if they want to talk
2. 3 Steps to getting feedback
   a. Listen Intently - tell them the truth if you can't
   b. Repeat it back in your own words - has no downside
   c. Thank them for the feedback and end the convo - you can always revisit later

"Listen intently and improve accordingly" - Dave

CHAPTER 10

THE STORM

I was not ready to put the instrument of pain back on my feet, but much to my surprise, the anguish was manageable. This was God sent, because our pace had almost doubled from my foolish looking duck walk. Dave had me take the lead again. Before we left, he had me double check that my rainproof pack cover was in an accessible spot. He had me show him where it was, and then he showed me where his was. I would soon find out why.

The sky went from blue with puffy white clouds to darkness in what felt like a matter of minutes. The wind was at our backs, and it felt cool. Part of enjoyed it, but the other part of me knew it was about to get miserable.

Dave tried to assure me. "Probably just a pop-up storm. Shouldn't last too long." I hoped he was right.

The first low rumble of thunder caused Dave and me

to look at each other. We were nearing the top of an incline, and you don't have to be a meteorologist to know that thunder doesn't occur without lightning.

As soon as we crested the top of the incline, the first drops of rain started to fall. It wasn't too bad to begin with. We paused for a moment and covered our packs with the rain gear. We didn't want to lose too much time, so we kept our packs on, and each took turns finding the rain gear and fitting the cover on the other person's pack. We got 400 more yards down-hill and the heavens opened. The only thought I had was, "will this day never end."

We hiked for another five minutes. You could tell Dave was looking for a spot to shield us from the deluge.

"Why don't we get under one of those large trees?" I suggested. It seemed logical to me.

Without breaking pace Dave replied, "You mean one of those tall wooden lightning rods?" I felt a moment of stupidity for even suggesting it. "Touché sir."

We caught a little break. The trail hugged a small rock outcropping to our right, and Dave no longer had to look for cover. He bee lined it for a small covered spot 20 feet off the trail.

The overhang was just large enough for us to drop our packs against the rock and for us to stand over them. The thunder grew now louder, and we could see flashes of lightning in the sky. I looked over to see Dave smiling.

"What are you smiling at?"

"Oh, I was just thinking how thankful I am that we have already crossed the river." We both laughed.

I had been wondering about something for a while and figured now was as good a time as any to ask. "Have you ever done one of these trips on your own?"

"A solo? Yea. Usually only for a night or two. They can be very impactful. Especially when you need to clear your head and refocus."

"I think I would like to do that one day." The words just came out of my mouth without thinking.

"I think you should." Dave said encouragingly. I don't know why, but I was surprised by his reply.

"You really think I could, after the whole boot debacle?"

Dave laughed. "Well I don't think you should next week. You might need a couple more trips under your belt before you are ready for something like that. But I'll be honest with you, I would much rather go with someone than go alone."

I thought that was interesting. "Really? Why?"

"I don't know exactly. I guess I enjoy bringing people along more than going it alone."

"Well that explains why you are such a good leader." It was not brown-nosing. Dave was the best leader I had ever seen. At that moment lightning filled the sky, and the boom of thunder followed suit.

After a moment, Dave said, "Leading people isn't easy. It takes a lot of work to know your people. Know when they need to be pushed and when they aren't ready. Constantly checking the temperature of the team. Knowing what your people's limits are as well as casting a vision for them beyond what they pictured for themselves."

"Kind of like bringing me out here."

"Exactly like bringing you out here. Most people think when you become a leader, you become the center of attention. That would be like going on this trip solo. In reality, that idea could not be further from the truth. When you become a leader, your people become the center of your attention. Their success is your success. John Maxwell puts it well, 'Being one step ahead makes you a leader. Being 50 steps ahead could make you a martyr.'"

I thought about that for a moment. I had always grown up thinking a leader is someone who charged out in front. Fearless and inspiring like William Wallace in the movie Braveheart. I never considered that being too far out front could be a bad thing.

I remembered a quote my dad used to say. "He who

thinks he leads, but has no followers, is only taking a walk."

The storm was passing. After a few more minutes, the sky started to clear and the sun came out, casting a shimmer of light on the trees as we hoisted our packs on for the remaining hike ahead.

Followers

1. Your followers should be the center of your attention

   a. Their success is your success.

2. If you are too far ahead, you are not a leader… you are a martyr.

3. A leader must:

   a. Know their people

      i. Strengths and weaknesses

      ii. Limits

   b. Have a vision for their people

      i. Beyond what they even see in themselves

   c. Take frequent temp checks

      i. Individually and team

CHAPTER 11

FIRE

No words sounded better to my ears than Dave's, "This looks like a good spot." With my feet problems and the freak storm, our day's journey was severely lengthened into the evening, prompting us to dawn our headlamps to finish the last leg. I had reached a new level of exhaustion. I was looking forward to a hot meal and a warm sleeping bag.

I went about my usual task of putting up the tent. By now it was becoming a rhythm, and I felt comfortable with the steps. As I pulled the final pieces from the packs, Dave surprised me by stepping in to help. With double the hands, the process was way more time efficient. I was thankful for the help, but curious why he wasn't working on the fire.

After the tent was done, Dave turned to me and said, "Wanna help me with the fire?" This was new. Suddenly I felt a little burst of energy at the thought.

"Sure."

"Great! It's going to take a little TLC because of the rain, but I think we can manage. Why don't you start looking for our starter supplies? We need a handful of each of these sizes. Smaller than a pencil, pencil, pinky finger, and thumb. When your done just put them next to the fire in their bundles. Remember, moisture is our enemy, so no live branches and no rotten ones."

Turning up the brightness on my headlamp I said, "I'm on it."

"Oh, one more thing. Since it rained, anything lying on the ground is not ideal. Try to find stuff under trees or hanging."

After a quick circle around our campsite, I managed to find a couple of honey holes for dry material. I remembered what Dave had said about rhododendron, so I steered clear of them. With the materials gathered and sorted, we both kneeled next to the fire ring Dave had assembled. I looked to Dave's right and saw a collection of larger pieces ready to go. How he built a ring and found larger logs remained a mystery to me.

Dave started his lesson. "Okay Paul, great job collecting. Making a fire requires three things; heat, fuel and oxygen." He pulled a match box out of his pocket and handed it to me. "This will be our initial source of heat. You have collected our fuel, and mother nature has provided oxygen, so we are ready to go."

Dave pulled out a bag of thin, dry, wood shavings from his pack and started to assemble them in something resembling a bird's nest. "This is going to be what we light with the match. As soon as it has lit, we will help it along with some oxygen until it has a good flame. Then we will start adding your materials from smallest to largest. Are you ready?"

I nodded and pulled out a match. Dave held the bird's nest in his hands and returned the nod. I struck the match, and the bright chemical flame burst into life. As quick as I could without extinguishing the flame, I held the match at an angle and brought it to Dave's hands. The dry nest slowly burned more and more. Dave held the nest close to his mouth and gently blew on it. Smoke billowed out the other end. After one more exhale, the nest burst into flames.

Dave placed it down in the center of the fire ring and grabbed a handful of twigs. "Now we don't want to smother it in twigs, but we don't want to have it die either." He carefully placed a few twigs on top of the burning nest and motioned for me to grab the rest. Gradually, the twigs began to burn as we added them one by one. The next few steps were logical. I reached over and started placing the larger sticks over the twigs. Dave applied a little man-made wind, and our fire slowly grew into life.

After we had a decent sized fire complete with larger logs, Dave turned to me and extended his hand. "Well done Paul. First fire?"

"Does a gas grill count?" We both laughed.

After Dave placed the pot of water over the flames, he sat back and said, "What experience do you have with self-development?"

I figured this was going to relate to a leadership lesson in some way. Now, at least I knew the subject. "Well . . . I keep up with my continued education credits, and the company has sent me to a couple of seminars over the years." I was grasping at straws.

"Okay . . ." Dave said with the tone that he was looking for more. "Let me ask this instead. What do you think of when you hear the term self-development?"

"I guess it means constantly improving yourself."

"I like the word 'constantly' Paul. That's a good working definition." You could tell Dave was passionate about this subject. "Your first answer is not uncommon. Most people make two mistakes in self-development. First, they gravitate toward the things they have to do to be good at their job. This is not really development, that is just doing good work. Second, they expect that it is the companies' job to develop them. Now a good company will develop its people, but unfortunately, not every company sees value in it."

"So really you are talking about what I am doing to better myself."

"That's right! Self development is a lot like making a fire. Do you remember the three elements of a fire?"

My exhausted brain was struggling to work. "Matches, wood and air?" was the best I could come up with.

Paul laughed. "Pretty close. Heat, fuel and oxygen are what I think you were going for. The heat we provided was a match, and that heat represents your desire to grow. Sometimes the desire comes easy, like a lighter, and sometimes it is hard, like a spark. Without it though, all you have is a bunch of wood." Dave smiled then continued. "The fuel represents the resources you use. You mentioned seminars. That is a great fuel for self-development. It could also be books you read, podcasts or any other type of resource that fuels the fire."

"What about a coach or mentor?"

"That is a great point, but a coach or mentor doesn't really feed the flames. What happened when I blew on the fire?"

"It burned hotter."

"Why do you think that is?"

I remembered the third element this time. "It added oxygen."

"You got it. Blowing on the fire adds more oxygen and accelerates burning. In the same way, bringing in a coach or mentor accelerates development."

"Okay so let me make sure I have it right. The fire starts with a spark and this is the moment that you have a desire to grow. That spark is nurtured into a flame by adding fuel and to accelerate the fire you add more oxygen which is like bringing in a coach or mentor. Does the size of fuel have anything to do with it?"

"What do you think?" Dave responded with a smile that said it did.

"Well you put the limbs on the fire in a specific order starting with the smaller ones. So maybe you should start small with your resources to gradually grow the fire?"

Dave nodded in agreement. "If you tried to light a big log after the small twigs, the fire would die before the logs could catch. If you have patience and gradually step up in size, the fire will be strong enough to burn. You are exactly right!" I could see the pride on Dave's face.

I had so many thoughts in my head about self-development and at the same time my mind was at capacity for the day. I needed to write this down and go to sleep. I decided to end our lesson for tonight.

"I'm going to need to sleep on this Dave, but not before I write it down."

Dave slowly got up and dusted off his pants. "There is one last thing I want to point out Paul. If you have any two of these things, you won't get a fire. Heat and oxygen but no fuel. Fuel and heat but no oxygen. Oxygen and fuel but no heat. It requires all three for self-development." And with that final word, Dave made his way to the tent.

Self Development

1. Like building a fire (must have all 3)
    a. Heat - the desire to develop and grow
    b. Fuel - resources that help (books, conferences, seminars, etc.)
        i. Add on small and grow over time
    c. Oxygen - coaches and mentors that help accelerate the growth
2. Doing your job is not development.
3. It is not the company's job to develop me, it is my responsibility.
4. It is a process to get the fire lit, but once it is going, the results can last and give you as much heat as you want.

CHAPTER 12

END OF THE TRAIL

I woke before the sun could peak through the trees. To my surprise, I looked over to find Dave still fast asleep. "Now it is my turn to be the ninja," I thought. I crept out of my sleeping bag as quietly as possible and stepped into the cool, crisp morning air.

The forest was just waking up, and I knew how I wanted to surprise Dave. I went straight to work gathering my supplies and trying to remember exactly what to do.

Dave crawled out of the tent to find a decent sized fire and two cups of steaming mocha coffee waiting. I was quite proud of myself, and for the first time, I felt like I had contributed something other than newbie mistakes. While it was just a fire and coffee, for the first time since Dave told me I would be replacing him as a leader, a part of me felt that I was ready. I was ready for the leadership.

After breakfast and a quick breakdown of camp, Dave and I went to work to 'leaving no trace'. I followed what I had seen Dave do for the fire. It felt like it took way more water than necessary, but after feeling for heat, I scattered the rocks in all different directions and finished just in time to see Dave sweeping the last section of the forest floor.

Dave and I stood back to survey our last campsite one last time.

"I can't thank you enough for giving me this experience Dave." I was feeling nostalgic in the moment. "It has truly been one that I will never forget."

"I couldn't have said it better, Paul." Dave reached in his pack and pulled out the map. I expected him to bring out the compass one last time. I secretly wanted to see the faded gold of the old device, but I was disappointed when he folded the map back and hoisted up his pack.

Our final leg was done in mostly silence. It was not difficult, but then again, compared to yesterday anything would be considered better.

I found myself being more aware of my surroundings: the sound of the birds in the trees, the swaying of the branches as the wind moved. I felt at peace. As we neared the end of the trail, reality started to sink in. The sound of cars moving along a road in the distance seemed to feel foreign and unwelcome to me.

As we reached the end of the trail, I found myself in a depressed mood. I did not want this time to end. I felt like there was so much more to learn. So many questions were not answered. To my surprise, Dave had one more new experience for me. Without saying a word, Dave made his way to the road and stuck out his right fist, thumb in the air.

"You want to hitchhike?" I said dumbfounded.

Dave looked at me with a coy smile and said, "unless you want to cross the river again."

I took my place next to him and reluctantly extended my arm. Yet another new experience. I was a hitchhiker.

CHAPTER 13

FINISH WELL

We got back to Dave's filthy Jeep thanks to a nice family with a truck. It was just as we had left it. In fact, there must have been years of mud on that thing because, the storm had done nothing to remove nature's paint. After a quick loading of the gear we were on our way back to civilization.

I made sure to remove my journal from my pack for the car ride home. There was so much to think about and evaluate. I kept racking my brain to make sure I had not missed something. Reading back through the pages brought back vivid memories. Some good. Some not so good. It was like walking through your childhood home and reliving all the memories from the different rooms.

I was reading through my notes following the boot catastrophe, when Dave interrupted my trip down memory lane.

"I have one final thing I would like to talk to you about Paul." I actually found myself relieved by his words. I was ready for more.

"What's that?" I asked.

"I want to talk to you about one of the most important things you can do as a leader."

I readied my pen. Determined not to miss a thing.

"I want to talk to you about leaving well."

I stopped halfway through the heading as I wrote it in my notebook. I did not want to talk about this. I was not ready to say goodbye to the best leader I had ever seen. Unfortunately, Dave had turned off his mind reading Jedi powers and continued on with the lesson.

"Eventually, the time will come when you will leave. It might be because you took a role at another company, or you got promoted to another division. It might even be something as crazy as retirement." Dave smiled while keeping his eyes on the road. "The one thing you should know is that everyone leaves. And when you do, you need to leave well."

I thought about stopping Dave there and telling him we could do this at another time. I did not want to have this conversation after all we had been through in the last four days, but something inside told me that this conversation wasn't just for me. This was just as much for him.

Dave continued, "A leader must always keep that in mind. And with that, they should always be preparing their people for their departure. Some people have an importance mentality as they leave. They hold on to important information and tasks right up until their departure. When they do leave, the gap that they create in the organization is not filled and can cripple the team. I refer to this person as an asset. . . not a leader. You see, a true leader is continually communicating and bringing people up to speed. They have a mindset of team. 'We go before ego' kind of thinking." I liked that quote, so I wrote it down.

"Another thing they do is constantly develop people who are independent thinkers. That way no single person is the linchpin to success. Every leader must filter their actions through a single question, 'What kind of legacy am I leaving?'. When you have a legacy mindset, the end of your time is much easier."

Dave must have understood that this was not easy for me to hear. As soon as I finished writing, he continued.

"Then it will come to your last week. It is really important to keep working, up to the last hour. Yes, hopefully there will be some celebration of your time. If you're lucky, there will be cake." Dave lifted his eyebrows a couple of times to solidify the hint. "But the last week of your time is just as, if not more, important than your first week. Make sure you hand off all the work. And most importantly, make sure you say goodbye to everyone. Some people will be easier than others for goodbyes, but it is important to include everyone. People need to hear you say goodbye." Dave nodded slowly and kept his eyes on the road. This was his final lesson.

I couldn't help thinking about how Dave must have felt as this chapter of his life was coming to a close. Was he sad? Nervous? Scared even?

Dave rolled down the window and let in some fresh air, wiping his cheek as he returned his hand to the wheel. In that moment I felt nothing but gratitude. Gratitude for all that he had given me from day one until now.

Finish Well

1. Everyone leaves eventually
2. A person who cannot leave without creating chaos is an asset, not a leader.
3. Continually be preparing your people for your departure
   a. Backfill your work
   b. Never be the sole knowledge holder
4. Continually ask the question "what kind of legacy do I want to leave?"
5. The last week is just as important as the first
   a. Keep working
   b. Hand off all remaining items
   c. Say "Goodbye" to everyone.

"We go before ego"

CHAPTER 14

SAYING GOODBYE

The time passed too quickly, but Dave practiced what he preached. He kept working up until his last hour. He handed off all the remaining responsibilities, cleaned out his office, and we had one heck of a going away party. I brought a large chocolate cake with Dave's face on the top.

I watched in awe as he went to each and every person. He looked them in the eye, shook their hands and said, "Goodbye for now." As the party wound down, I slipped past the crowd. I wasn't nervous about saying goodbye to Dave, but I wasn't looking forward to it either.

I was in my new office, Dave's old one, when I heard a soft knock at the door. The time had come. It was my turn. Dave stood in the doorway for a moment. Probably taking in the space one last time. His eyes made their way around the room and finally rested on me.

"Paul, I am so excited for you. I know you will do great things, but more important than that, I know you will be a great leader. It has been one of my greatest pleasures to be a part of your journey my friend. I wish you the best." He reached out and shook my hand with a smile on his face. "Goodbye for now." With that, he turned and walked through the door for the last time.

I sat there for a long stretch, thinking about the shoes I had to fill. . . more like hiking boots. As I was smiling at myself for the joke, something caught my eye on the end of the desk. A small brown box with the name "Paul" written in marker on the top. I reached out and opened the lid to find the worn golden compass nestled in paper shreds. I smiled to myself. Jedi. As I held the compass in my hands, I noticed something etched in the worn metal.

"TO ALWAYS FIND YOUR WAY"

EPILOGUE

Paul led at the company for many years. He made mistakes. More mistakes than he would like to admit, but he was loved by his people and continued to lead them every step of the way. He and Dave are still friends to this day. Paul was with the company for another ten years before finally landed the contract he dreamed of. In three short months, he and a select team will venture abroad to create the division that will forever change the name of the company to Aeromic Aviation International.

Paul knocked on the half-opened door and let himself in before hearing the reply. Kevin, Rebecca and Pat were hunched over a large conference table studying an array of data and models.

Kevin spoke up first. "I would say come in but. . ."

Paul smiled as he leaned against the markerboard at the end of the glass conference room. "I see you are all hard at work. You wouldn't happen to be looking at the latest model of the M77."

Pat thought, "What are you? Some kind of Jedi?" but didn't vocalize it.

Kevin shuffled some of the project papers wondering how Paul knew that was exactly what they were discussing. "Yea. It is going to be an interesting endeavor. What's up?"

Paul's grin widened, and all three could tell there was a glimmer of something was in his eyes. "I have some exciting news folks, but before I tell you, I have to ask you a question."

It was Rebecca who spoke up this time. "Exciting news huh? I'm intrigued! What's the question?"

"Have any of you ever been backpacking?"

ABOUT THE AUTHOR

Luke Crane is the owner and principal consultant for Leadership Cohort LLC. In addition to his work as an author, Luke consults and speaks on various topics relating to leadership, teamwork and effectiveness in the workplace. He has a deep passion for leadership and watching others win.

Leadership Cohort is a consulting firm that specializes in entry level leaders. They understand that the first few years of leadership are instrumental in leadership. For companies, being intentional about leadership development within the organization is paramount. Leadership Cohort partners with companies to create comprehensive plans to grow and mature their leadership pipeline.

Leadership Cohort offers the following professional services:

Team Workshops

Consulting Services

Online Courses

Speaking Service

To learn more about Luke and Leadership Cohort, please visit www.leadershipcohort.com. If you'd like to contact Luke directly, he can be reached at luke@leadershipcohort.com.

Made in the USA
Columbia, SC
11 November 2019

83092610R00061